August 28, 1989

For Katie, on her very "special day." When she really is legally part of our family.

With love,
Nana & Grandpa

First edition for the United States, Canada, and
the Philippines published 1987 by Barron's
Educational Series, Inc.
First published 1987 by Piccadilly Press Ltd.,
London, England
Illustrations © Cathie Shuttleworth, 1987

All inquiries should be addressed to:
Barron's Educational Series, Inc.
113 Crossways Park Drive
Woodbury, New York 11797
Library of Congress Catalog Card No. 86-26623
International Standard Book No. 0-8120-5805-4

Library of Congress Cataloging-in-Publication Data
Howitt, Mary Botham, 1799-1888.
  The spider and the fly.
  Summary: An illustrated version of the well-known
poem about the wily spider and the luckless fly. Includes
an addendum with a modern-day example of why it is best
not to trust strangers who offer treats.
  1. Spiders--Juvenile poetry. 2. Flies--Juvenile
poetry. 3. Children's poetry, English.   [1. Spiders--
Poetry. 2. Flies--Poetry. 3. Conduct of life--Poetry.
4. English poetry   ] I. Shuttleworth, Cathie, ill.
II. Title.
PR4809.H2S64 1987   821'.8   86-26623
ISBN 0-8120-5805-4

Printed in Hong Kong

Cathie Shuttleworth lives in Surrey, although she
is Suffolk born. She studied art in Ipswich and Surrey, training in calligraphy, heraldry and illumin-
ation, and after deciding not to become a medieval
monk she specialised in children's illustration.
However she did draw the heraldry on the official
programme for the wedding of HRH Prince
Andrew and Sarah Ferguson.

With special thanks to Ruth Shuttleworth for the
addendum.

The SPIDER and the FLY

by Mary Howitt
illustrated by Cathie Shuttleworth

BARRON'S
Woodbury, New York · Toronto

"Will you walk into my parlor?"
    said the Spider to the Fly,
"'Tis the prettiest little parlor
    that ever you did spy.
The way into my parlor
    is up a winding stair,
And I have many curious things
    to show when you are there."

"Oh no, no," said the little Fly,
  "to ask me is in vain,
For who goes up your winding stair
  can ne'er come down again."

"I'm sure you must be weary, dear,
    with soaring up so high;
Will you rest upon my little bed?"
    said the Spider to the Fly.
"There are pretty curtains drawn around,
    the sheets are fine and thin,
And if you like to rest awhile,
    I'll snugly tuck you in!"

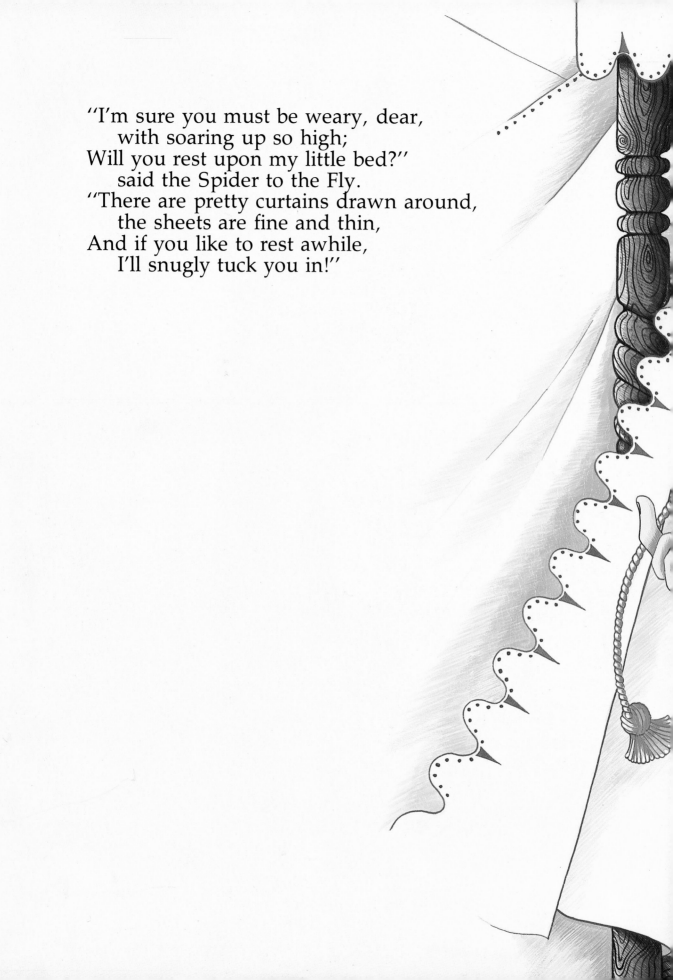

"Oh no, no," said the little Fly,
   "for I've often heard it said,
They never, never wake again,
   who sleep upon your bed!"

Said the cunning Spider to the Fly,
   "Dear friend, what can I do,
To prove the warm affection
   I've always felt for you?
I have within my pantry
   good store of all that's nice
I'm sure you're very welcome —
   will you please to take a slice?"

"Oh no, no," said the little Fly,
   "kind sir, that cannot be,
I've heard what's in your pantry and
   I do not wish to see."

"Sweet creature," said the Spider,
    "you're witty and you're wise;
How handsome are your gauzy wings,
    how brilliant are your eyes!
I have a little looking-glass
    upon my parlor shelf,
If you'll step in a moment, dear,
    you shall behold yourself."

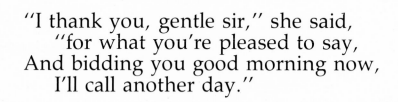

"I thank you, gentle sir," she said,
  "for what you're pleased to say,
And bidding you good morning now,
  I'll call another day."

The Spider turned him round about
    and went into his den,
For well he knew the silly Fly
    would soon come back again.
So he wove a subtle web,
    in a little corner sly,
And set his table ready,
    to dine upon the Fly.

Then he came out to his door again
    and merrily did sing:
"Come hither, hither, pretty Fly,
    with the pearl and silver wing.
Your robes are green and purple —
    there's a crest upon your head;
Your eyes are like the diamond bright,
    but mine are dull as lead."

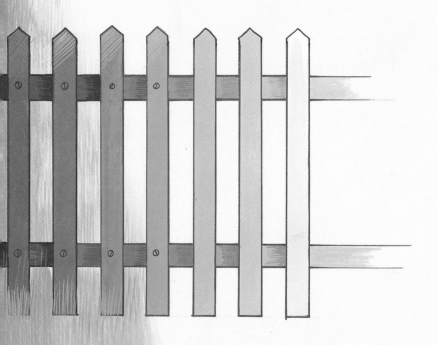

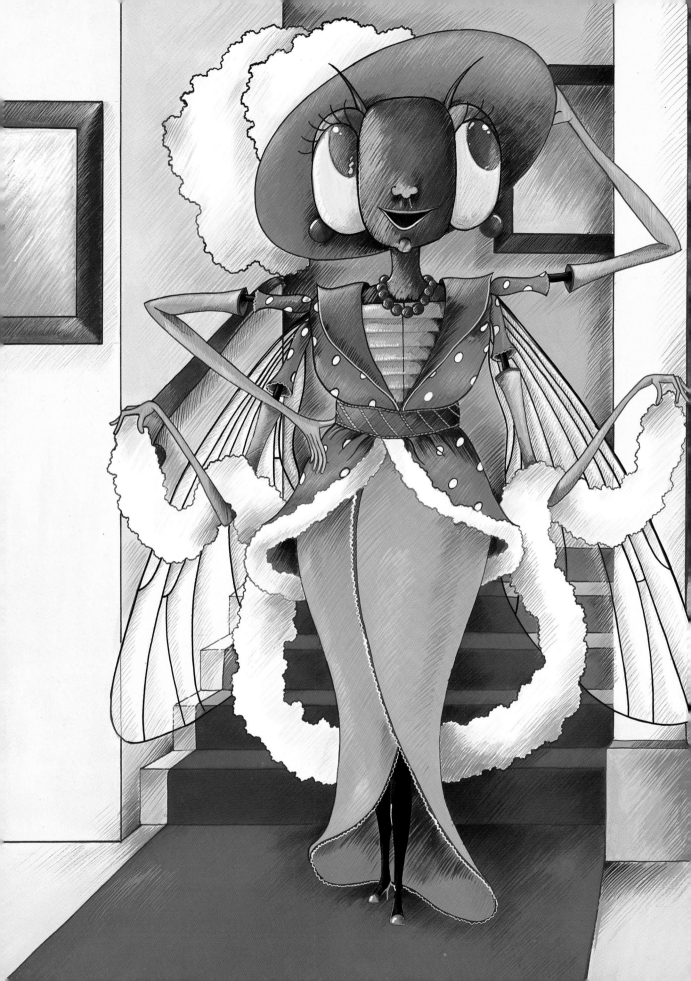

Alas, alas! How very soon
    this silly little Fly,
Hearing his wily, flattering words,
    came slowly flitting by.
With buzzing wings she hung aloft,
    then near and nearer drew,
Thinking only of her brilliant eyes,
    and green and purple hue;
Thinking only of her crested head —
    poor foolish thing!

Up jumped the cunning Spider
    and fiercely held her fast.
He dragged her up his winding stair,
    into his dismal den,
Within his little parlor —
    but she ne'er came out again!

"Will you come into my sports car?"
    said the kind man to the boy.
"'Tis the fastest little sports car
    that you ever did enjoy.
You can sit upon the front seat
    as a very special treat.
I will buy you an ice-cream,
    and what's your favorite sweet?"
"Oh no, no," said the little boy,
    "to ask me is in vain,
For who goes in your sports car,
    may ne'er see friends again."

Oh, clever little Johnny,
    and you be wise, Jane, too.
Don't put your trust in strangers,
    however kind to you.
Don't take their sweets or toys or coins,
    however hard they try.
Remember the sad, sad tale of
    the Spider and the Fly.